FAITH THAT CAN MOVE MOUNTAINS

DR. JAMES T. JACKSON

FAITH THAT CAN MOVE MOUNTAINS

DR. JAMES T. JACKSON

MEWE
Lithonia, GA

© 2024 James T. Jackson

All rights reserved.

No part of this publication may be reproduced, stored in a retrieval system, or transmitted in any form or by any means, electronic, mechanical, photocopying, recording, or otherwise, without the expressed written permission of the publisher.

Scripture references are taken from various versions and translations of the Holy Bible. Pronouns for referring to the Father, Son, and Holy Spirit are capitalized intentionally and the words satan and devil are never capitalized.

Publisher:
MEWE, LLC
www.mewellc.com

First Edition
ISBN: 979-8-9871970-8-0

Library of Congress Control Number: 2024906493

Printed in the United States of America.

To my dear wife, Richarda Jackson, your love and support have empowered me to complete this work.

To the Saints of the New Jerusalem Church of Jesus Christ, Danville IL., whom I love dearly.

To these Saints, who molded and strengthened my faith in God's awesome power to accomplish anything, I must call out by name: my mother-in-law, Evangelist Della Stewart, Deacon Levi Coleman, Mother Marie Coleman, Sister Amelia Coleman, Deacon Jimmy Stevenson, Sister Grace Stevenson, and Mother Lena Price.

TABLE OF CONTENT

Acknowledgments ix

Foreword – Dr. Ruth W. Smith xi

Foreword – Dr. Jerry L. Wilson xv

Introduction xix

Chapter 1 – Defining Faith 1

Chapter 2 – Old Saints Bootcamp 11

Chapter 3 – Overcoming Doubt 23

Chapter 4 – Spending Time with God 31

Chapter 5 – Faith in Action 41

Chapter 6 – The Science of Faith 51

Chapter 7 – Enduring Faith 57

Chapter 8 – Living a Life of Faith 63

Chapter 9 – Possessing High Impact Faith 69

Chapter 10 – Faith that Demands Opposition 75

Chapter 11 – Wonderous Faith 83

Endnotes 89

About the Author 91

ACKNOWLEDGEMENTS

I would like to thank the Power of Faith International church family for their wholehearted encouragement and support during the writing process. I would also like to thank a group of "Special Friends" with whom I was able to bounce ideas and debate scriptural interpretations that widened my perspective.

FOREWORD

What is faith? How can we maximize the benefits of faith in our personal walk? What can abundant faith achieve in the life of a believer?

These and many more questions are explored in this important masterpiece, ***Faith That Can Move Mountains***. Dr. James T. Jackson explains faith in a clear and instructive way, guiding readers on how having strong faith can help them live their lives with purpose as believers. This book offers step-by-step guidance for believers on how to develop a deep and meaningful faith in the Lord.

Life can be tough, and those challenges can sometimes shake our faith. But it's precisely in those moments that we need faith the most. While we can't control everything that happens to us in this life, we can control how we react to it. Having a deep and meaningful faith tied to our purpose in Christ will help to ensure that we grow stronger from the trials of life instead of allowing them to tear us apart.

Abundant faith fuels us and helps us to grow, no matter the circumstances of life. Dr. Jackson has experienced this truth in his own life, and eagerly shares it in a way that resonates with readers at every stage of their own personal faith journey. The wisdom he shares is timeless, biblically accurate, and transformative.

Throughout this book, Dr. Jackson equips believers with the tools necessary to navigate life with purpose and conviction. Just as a tiny seed grows into a mighty tree with the right care and attention, so too does faith require cultivation and nurturing. By drawing upon his own experiences and the wisdom of God's Word, Dr. Jackson offers hope and encouragement to those navigating their spiritual journey.

If you embrace the teachings in this book, your faith will grow immensely, and your connection with God will deepen. I highly recommend this book to anyone seeking a spiritual life rooted in faith and longing to witness the impossible become possible in their lives. Dr. Jackson writes from personal experience and is well-equipped to provide such guidance, as he not only teaches the Word of God but also lives it out in his own life.

Ultimately, ***Faith That Can Move Mountains*** is a roadmap for believers seeking to enhance their connection with God. By following Dr. Jackson's guidance and following the principles outlined in this book, readers can experience a profound transformation in their relationship with God and live with a newfound sense of purpose and conviction.

Dr. Ruth W Smith
Archbishop
Light of the World
Covenant Fellowship, Int'l

FOREWORD

Now faith is the substance of things hoped for and the evidence of things not seen. For by it the elders obtained a good report ... But without faith it is impossible to please Him: for he that cometh to God must believe that he is, and that he is a rewarder of them that diligently seek Him (Hebrews 11:1-2, 6).

Dr. James T. Jackson explores the most critical aspects of faith in his new book, ***Faith That Can Move Mountains***. He writes on how faith can transform our lives, highlighting the importance of belief and action. Transformation is the only true way to accomplish real change in relationships, financial status, and any other meaningful life dynamics. Dr. Jackson lays out the blueprint for how it's done!

Faith and action work together to produce the results that we desire. Faith is the belief, trust, and confidence we have in God. It's the inner conviction that a desired outcome is possible or achievable through our relationship with God. Faith also provides the motivation and inspiration necessary to pursue our purpose in Christ. When we have faith in

God, it gives us the courage to take action even when faced with uncertainty or challenges.

Action refers to the practical steps, efforts, or behaviors we undertake to embrace the purpose God has prepared for our lives. It involves planning, decision-making, and actively engaging in activities that move us closer to our goals. Action transforms our beliefs and intentions into tangible reality through faith. Without action, faith remains dormant and ineffective.

So, if you want to impact the world for Christ, this is definitely a must-read. Throughout this book, Dr. Jackson demonstrates how faith empowers us to overcome any obstacle in life and realize the fullness of the potential God has placed within us. When we experience a genuine, transformative relationship with God, nothing can prevent us from living out the purpose God has called us to.

Faith That Can Move Mountains is a clarion call to believers to embrace a life of faith and action for the cause of God's Kingdom. This book aims to equip readers with confidence and conviction so they can dream big and receive the abundant blessings promised to those who diligently seek the Lord.

It's time for us all to realize the God-given potential within us and change the world for God's Kingdom! Each one of us has a role to play in God's perfect plan, and through Faith that Can Move Mountains, Dr. Jackson helps guide us in embracing the mission that only we can accomplish in this world.

Dr. Jerry L. Wilson
Senior Pastor
Salem Baptist Church
Champaign, IL

INTRODUCTION

> *If we were going to have a name like "Power of Faith," then we were certainly going to have to understand how to harness that "Power."*

After a successful two-and-a-half-year-old church merger, one that was certain to produce a how-to book and a wave of new church mergers, a scandal erupted out of nowhere. It took place among the leadership and threatened the newly formed and thriving congregation with the derailing of the merger. Without warning, the scandal thrust me into a position that totally compromised my pastoral and ethical values. My painful option was only one: to expose the failings of someone I loved and considered a friend and a mentor. To do so would ultimately disrupt the harmony of the church and cause a split within the congregation.

To make matters worse, I had no time to figure out the best possible way for me to smooth over the failings to protect reputations because the church was facing an impending deadline that was critical to its survival.

God had put me in a position where I and another minister would have to take a stand. That stand would not only make us unpopular, but it would also shake the church, especially the faith of the many new babes in Christ that had been added over the last few years. The position I was thrust into made me feel sick and perplexed and shook the very foundation of my faith.

The pressure was on, and I felt as if things had been taken out of my control. I certainly had to act prayerfully and quickly. At stake for me was to do the right thing and walk away from the friend and ministry that I had given so much to and come to love. I would surrender all and do the only thing I could, which was to act responsibly by bringing the incriminating information to the forefront and try to do some degree of damage control.

As I expected, the information caused an uproar, and a split in the congregation seemed inevitable. In an effort to minimize the fall-out, I tried to simply remove myself from the situation, leaving all of the hard-fought gains and assets with the congregation. So, I simply walked away without objection.

That separation from the congregation left me broken and exhausted. My heart and spirit hurt especially for the many babes in Christ that I had brought into the congregation and left behind. Not only was my faith bruised, but I had resolved to stop pastoring for a while and lick my wounds while I pursued my Ph.D.

In my mind, I was the one responsible for taking my former congregation into a merger that produced a split – that was heart-breaking. My pride took a beating as well. Three years of hard work wasted, not to mention the personal sacrifices and resources that I had invested—all down the drain. All I could do was hang my head and walk away, never to look back. That was on a Wednesday…but by Sunday, there I was holding an organizational meeting for a new congregation.

A Change of Course

How could it be that I was involved with this organizational meeting when I was not going to even consider pastoring for a while? Well, I was reluctant, until the babes in Christ began calling and insisting that I could not simply abandon them with no place to go. They started raising money for the new meeting place, and at warp speed, we were in a fully furnished worship facility complete with training rooms. Joining us was a skeletal crew of less than 15 members who wanted to continue to grow in Christ and develop their faith.

From my perspective, the meeting did not start out as the organization meeting it was meant to be — an opportunity to give the babes some direction. Instead, I was trying to identify some ministries that would provide the needed nurturance with a strong biblical base that could provide the healing these hurting ones would need. The irony was that I was the one who was hurting the most and also needed healing.

The meeting turned out to be an organizational meeting for the new ministry. These young members in Christ were resolved to continue the wonderful work we were doing and were excited to be out from under the restrictions of the formal traditional ministry we had just left. We were not a congregation formally, but these trusting souls were trying to pick a name for the ministry that would describe who we were and what we wanted to convey to the world. We were all dealing with some degree of uncertainty and church hurt but what was certain to these new believers was that God had put us together for the new work. Their faith was intact and on the go.

Of course, there was the expected excitement and anxiety of starting a new chapter in our Christian walk while suffering the loss of many of our former church family. Little did I know that something powerful was about to take place. I was about to collide with the scripture, *"Lord I believe, help thou mine unbelief."*

As I listened to the vision of the people whom I considered still young in Christ, I discovered that what they had laid hold of was true MOUNTAIN-MOVING FAITH (See Mark 9:24).

Faith to Live By

The Bible speaks of seven different kinds of faith: little faith, great faith, wavering faith, blind faith, substantive faith, empty faith, and saving faith. I call this collection the "total faith package." I'd like to say that theological training over many years of studying the bible and pastoring had revealed the "total package" to me, but that was not the case. I had preached many messages on faith but never in a series.

As I embarked on my quest to fulfill my pastoral obligations, I wanted to ensure that the church family understood how to live up to its name. If we were going to have a name like "Power of Faith," then we were certainly going to have to understand how to harness that "Power." So, I sprinkled faith messages and studies throughout the course of the first year.

It was gratifying at times when the congregation was faced with challenges, how one of the members would say something like "We'll have to believe we are the power of faith" or "We just have to use our faith." It was those statements that began to challenge me to examine my personal faith according to how the Bible sees it.

I was quite sure that I had mountain-moving faith. Hadn't I laid hands on the sick and they had recovered, and built four other churches? Believe me, that takes faith!

Certainly, anyone who had been preaching the gospel since the age of seventeen and had pastored since the age of nineteen—that's over forty years of ministry—must be able to move mountains with their faith! Or so I thought. But each time a statement about faith was made by one of the babes who looked to me for guidance, it would cause me to examine my own faith stance.

As the leader, I was simply trying to help my young congregation understand the way God moves. But, to my astonishment, I found that in reality, it was the "rookies" of my church who were teaching me how God really moves! What I finally realized was that years of church had blurred the lines between true faith and "unrealistic expectations."

Unrealistic Expectations

"Unrealistic expectations" are those that place the burden of proof solely in the hands of God while you sit and watch. It's like trying to buy a car with no money and no job. When we look at our own reality in comparison with the sphere of what we need God to do in our lives, we have already limited the outcome. Yes, we believe that true faith is not at all predicated on any tangible thing from us other than what we believe about God. We hold on to

Corinthians 2:5, *"… that your faith should not stand in the wisdom of men, but in the power of God."* But don't let that confuse you. Although faith relies on what you believe about God, it still requires your input. For instance, it would be a lapse in true faith to ask and believe God for rain and leave your umbrella at home. James 5:4 says, *"Yea, a man may say, Thou hast faith, and I have works: shew me thy faith without thy works, and I will shew thee my faith by my works."* I heard a saying years ago and have held on to it ever since: "Wishing and hoping can't change your fate; God will provide the fish but you must dig the bait!"

All too often when I counsel God's people, they make an admission of their lack of faith. The reality is not that they lacked faith or that God did not answer, but simply that they expected God to provide and do all the work as well. You see, faith is always followed by its corresponding works. *"But wilt thou know, O vain man, that faith without works is dead?"* (James 2:20). When we really believe that God is going to do something, we should get busy laying the groundwork for the blessings we expect.

It would be foolish to believe in God for a house and not go looking at houses and talking to lenders.

Along the way, you could be challenged with credit issues, but, as you talk to the lenders, you begin to work on the credit issues they raise. It is often the issues raised that challenge our faith. Some people will simply give up when a challenge comes up but, when you believe in God, you will begin to address those obstacles. Faith is our fuel for action that brings to reality the substance of the things we believe God for. If you want a garden, then you plant some seeds and water them, all the while waiting and looking for the sprouts to come up.

Now, whenever a saint of God questions their faith, what they are really saying is that they are not sure how their interests line up with the Word and will of God. When we are sure that the things we are seeking God for are in His will, then that is the beginning of mountain-moving faith. On the other hand, when our request seems to be self-serving, we only "hope" that God will grant our petition. It is this "hope" that we equate with a lack of faith when it's really a question of not being in His will.

Hebrews 11:6 states, *"But without faith it is impossible to please him; for he that cometh to God must believe that he is, and that he is a rewarder of them that diligently seek him."* When we spend our time seeking the Lord through ministers or ministries, in prayer lines and workshops, what we get is a *"zeal of God but not according to knowledge"* (Romans 10:2).

Let's dig deeper into what the Bible calls faith.

Dr. James T. Jackson

CHAPTER 1

Defining Faith

> *Faith is your belief acted out with human capital or an investment of effort based on your expectation from God.*

All religious traditions and belief systems have some measure of faith. When we are speaking about their faith or the faith of an individual as their central operating system, we are looking at trust in a higher power or a spiritual force that transcends the material world. This trust is often rooted in personal convictions or traditions and can provide a sense of comfort and purpose to individuals.

But what exactly is biblical faith, and why is it so different?

Biblical Faith

Biblical faith is not purely spiritual. Without a natural agency, it would be God working a miracle on His own and not requiring our input at all. *"Even so faith, if it hath not works, is dead, being alone"* (James 2:17). The apostle James introduces the human outworking of faith, which is action. If you believe that God is working on your behalf, then you should make the necessary preparations to receive the blessing. One example I often give when teaching on faith is that it starts with the assurance of scripture. Scripture asserts that you can say to the mountain:

> *Be thou removed, and be thou cast into the sea: and shall not doubt in his heart, but shall believe that those things which he saith shall come to pass: he shall have whatsoever he saith* (Mark 11:23).

What it is saying is that if you put in the work, you will see progress because faith without works is dead.

Simply start and watch the mountain diminish as you cast it into yonder sea. If you just pick up a handful of the mountain, someone will come along with a shovel and help you, and, before you know it, someone will be there with a bulldozer, and the mountain will move. Here I am speaking metaphorically. Faith is your belief acted out with human capital or an investment of effort based on your expectation from God.

The statement, *"Faith without works is dead"* essentially means that true faith is not merely a matter of intellectual assent or profession, but must be demonstrated through one's actions and behavior. In other words, if a person claims to have faith but their actions do not reflect that faith, then their faith is incomplete and "dead." Simply standing in an elevator saying to yourself that it can take you to the third floor will not get you there unless you press the right button.

James 2:26 uses the analogy of a body without a spirit to illustrate this point: *"For as the body without the spirit is dead, so faith without works is dead also."* True faith should inspire good works and righteous behavior since the two are inseparable. Therefore, it is not enough to simply say that you believe in something: you must also live it out in your words and deeds.

So, faith is not just a feel-good state about something, or vaguely hoping for it. Rather, it is an assurance of something that we are confident will happen, even if we cannot see it or understand how it will come about.

DEFINING FAITH

The writer of Hebrews offers a definition of faith that speaks to substantiating our hope: *"Now faith is the assurance of things hoped for, the conviction of things not seen"* (Hebrews 11:1 ESV). This definition of faith is powerful because it tells us what faith is and what it is not.

To fully understand this verse, it's helpful to look at the original Greek. The word for "substance" is hypostasis, which can also be translated as "assurance" or "confidence." It carries the idea of a firm foundation or strong support. This means that faith is not just a feeling or an abstract concept; no, it's a solid, though intangible, foundation upon which we can base our lives. Think of the struts that undergird the foundation of a bridge and you have a concrete picture.

The Greek root word for "hoped" is elpizo, which means "to hope for" or "to expect." It implies a confident supposition, as against wishful thinking. When we have faith, we have a confident expectation that what we hope for will come to pass.

The word for "evidence" is elegchos, which can also be translated as "proof" or "conviction." It carries the idea of something that is certain or indisputable. Faith provides us with conviction and certainty that the things we cannot see are nonetheless real and true. This evidence is like having a layaway receipt. With a layaway receipt, you don't have the items that are laid away, and you cannot see them until you are finished paying for them. However, the very fact that they are listed on the receipt gives you a certain confidence that the items exist and that they will be yours once paid for. In the same way, when we trust the evidence of our faith, we have the confidence that, once the prayers are sent up, the blessings will come down.

When we put all of these Greek words together, we see that faith is a solid foundation, a confident expectation, and a certain conviction of things we cannot see. This means our faith is not blind, but rather it is based on a firm foundation of trust and assurance in the character of God. We believe that He is faithful, He will never lie, and that all His promises are yes and amen. We believe that He honors His Word, and He answers faith-filled prayers and declarations. We believe that He cares for us, has good plans for us, and will never leave us nor forsake us. This allows us to confidently hope for and expect the promises of God to come to pass, even when we have yet to see them.

So, Hebrews 11:1 offers a powerful definition of faith, but the chapter doesn't stop there. It presents what is often referred to as the "Hall of Faith," where are listed many individuals from the Old Testament who demonstrated remarkable faith in God. These heroes from Abel to Rahab are celebrated for their unshakeable trust in God, even in the face of peril. By studying their stories and understanding how faith worked in them, we can learn how to cultivate a strong and enduring faith in our own lives.

Hebrews 11:6 goes on to offer further insight into the pre-eminence of faith, stating that *"without faith it is impossible to please God, because anyone who comes to him must believe that he exists and that he rewards those who earnestly seek him"* (NIV). This verse tells us that our believing that God exists and seeking a deeper connection with Him is at the heart of biblical faith. When we trust in God and seek Him wholeheartedly, we can experience a sense of fulfillment and purpose that transcends our mountains of struggle and indecision. This is not to say that faith is a panacea for all of life's problems, but rather that it can provide a firm grounding and pathway to navigating difficult times.

The above verse goes on to say that God rewards those who earnestly seek Him. This does not necessarily mean material blessings or earthly success. Rather, it suggests that when we seek God with all our heart, we will find Him, and experience the rewards He is pleased to give us. This leads to a peace and fulfillment that cannot be found anywhere else.

In this way, faith is not simply a belief system or a set of practices. It is a way of life. It is a way of orienting ourselves towards God and adjusting our view of the world with Him as the focal point. Even the smallest amount of faith can have a tremendous impact on our lives.

Miracles Produced by Faith

Throughout history, there have been countless examples of individuals who have accomplished remarkable feats through the power of their faith. From Moses parting the Red Sea to David defeating Goliath, these stories demonstrate the power of faith to overcome humanly insurmountable obstacles.

DEFINING FAITH

Likewise, faith has produced miracles in the lives of individuals and communities in our present day. Whether it's physical healing or profound revelation, miracles attest to the power of faith and the grace of God. As a pastor, I have seen the power of God save the lives of many who trust in Him. I have been at the hospital when doctors informed the family that there was nothing else that could be done to help a loved one. But the Bible says that *"the prayer of faith shall save the sick"* (James 5:15). After such prayers were made, I have seen those same people totally recover. Some call it a miracle; I simply call it the power of faith.

Of course, it's important to note that faith alone is not enough to accomplish great things or create miracles. Action and effort are also required to bring about meaningful change. When we combine faith with action, we can tap into a powerful dynamic that can help us overcome the impossible.

In the next chapter, I will tell you what I learned about faith from my church community.

CHAPTER 2

Old Saints Bootcamp

> *They taught me that faith is not confined to the walls of the church but that faith informs the life and actions of the believer.*

I'd like to take you on a journey through my early days as a young pastor that I like to call my "church bootcamp experience." We will see parallels between this experience and the example of dedicated senior members with their profound faith. These remarkable individuals, whom we affectionately called "saints," served as an inspiration for all who witnessed their deeply rooted trust in God, even in the midst of the most challenging of circumstances.

Imagine entering a church as a teenage preacher, surrounded by seasoned saints who towered over my youthful stature like great oak trees! Young and inexperienced as I was, I was afforded the highest level of respect and love, simply because they did not question God's appointment of me as their pastor.

What struck me was the profound spiritual serenity of these seniors, which showed me how to trust God in all weathers.

Trailblazers in the Faith

As a novice pastor, like Paul's disciple, Timothy, I found myself both leading and being led by these senior members whose faith shone like a beacon of light over rocky shoals. To me, they embodied the very essence of what it means to trust God in the best and worst of times.

One particular elder stands out among the saints. She was Mother Maria Coleman—a woman who, despite a debilitating sickness, consistently put aside her troubles and attended church service all the days of her life. Her ailment was severe to the point of losing a limb, yet her determination to worship and trust God remained solid as a rock. There were many times when Mother Coleman could do no more than make it to the church's vestibule and call for me, Elder Jackson, to come and pray. In the face of her trust and expectation, I could not help but pray the effectual fervent prayer of faith. When I prayed for such a woman who was depending on God's mercy, I would beg God to come through for Mother. You see, Mother's need tugged at my mind and emotions so much that I prayed with both spirit and soul. It was, in fact, the prayer training ground for me as I learned to pray precisely focused on the seriousness of the need with all my heart and my emotions for what I believed from the Word of God. Witnessing her faith, I couldn't help but be in awe of her resolute spirit. It left no room for me to do anything but get on board and bind my faith with hers, tethered to the trustworthy Word of God.

That's how these saints became my trailblazers. Led by apostolic champion Deacon Levi Coleman, I was guided through some of the most daunting faith challenges—as we'll see shortly. He and the other saints taught me valuable lessons about faith, resilience, and unyielding trust in God's Word as the final authority, even when there was no solution in sight.

One Heart, One Mind

I remember shortly after God had put us together, I was faced with leading one group of seniors from the Church of God faith and another group of seniors from the Apostolic church faith. How do you work with two denominationally and culturally different groups in the same sanctuary? Here were two of the most conservative groups with no one below the age of seventy-eight, the only youngsters being my wife, our children, and myself.

I remember once seeking the advice of Deacon Coleman about dealing with the doctrinal differences between the two groups. Because he was such a stern man, I was expecting a no-nonsense answer to the question that would certainly exclude those with opposing views to his. To my surprise, Deacon looked at me and asked if I had the Holy Ghost. Once I answered yes, Deacon, in a matter-of-fact way underscored by his sharp wit simply said, "Ask Him," and walked away. Boy, what a simple but profound lesson!

Shortly after that encounter, I was certain that God would give me a directive that would consolidate the two faiths into one coherent group of Bible-directed saints. To accomplish this goal of making two congregations one, we would have to move the congregation to a new facility and change the name of the church. There were many problems with this initiative.

First, the smaller groups of Church of God members were not very cooperative and understandably protective of their traditional ways. Secondly, we did not have many members, and unless the two groups cooperated, we would not have any money and would probably lose a few members.

Every time I went into prayer, I was certain that the directive of God was clear. At nineteen, I had no real money, I knew little about credit, and to top it all, we were in a conservative lending community—if you know what I mean. A nineteen-year-old African American pastor with a few old folks with no money trying to—get this!—buy a church, not rent one.

But in faith with zero practical experience, I launched a building fund and saw faith go to work. The congregation stepped up to the plate. I was not aware of Deacon Coleman's love for cooking or his popularity. He started selling sweet potato pies and peach cobblers. I thought to myself, "You can't buy no church with potato pies; you need money!" One day I unwittingly said it out aloud, and didn't all hell break loose! Deacon was hurt, not by my words, but by my lack of faith. He told me that if I didn't believe God could do it, I needed to quit right then and there. With his customary wit, he added, "It takes a penny to make a dollar." He told me that if I believed that my vision was from God, I needed to trust Him and find a place for our new church. We had already decided on the new name, "New Jerusalem Church of Jesus Christ."

Long story short, as we exercised our faith, so did it happen! Within the next year, we would buy not only a church but the house next door, the parking lot, the apartment building, the house behind the church, a church van, and a bus! We launched the first-ever television ministry in our community and a minority news publication in the city of Danville, IL. And to top it all, the church from whom we purchased the building paid our mortgage for the first year as they needed to rent space while their building was being prepared. Ain't God good—I mean, ain't God good?

Just as a campfire serves as a central gathering point, where stories are shared and hearts are warmed, the combined faith of the saints became a source of encouragement and inspiration for all.

Their unwavering belief in God's faithfulness and goodness reminds us that, no matter how fierce the storms, there is always a firm foundation on which to anchor our faith. It is noteworthy that the saints' confidence that Christ was working on their side was fully based on the relationship of holiness and God's promises. There was a comfort in knowing beyond a shadow of a doubt that one's assurance of salvation entitled one to the rights of sonship. Now that is true faith!

As I spent time with the saints during church bootcamp, I latched on to their firm trust in God's promises through His Word. Their prayers and implicit faith during prayer meetings in times of great need would reverberate through my spirit during my formative years as a pastor at church bootcamp.

The saints' commitment to the Word of God, intermingled with whatever was rustling around in the background, only seemed to produce more faith. It was woven through the favorite song of Mother Grace, "If I had ten thousand tongues, I'd praise Him with everyone." There was Sister Price, who never left her tambourine behind on her way "to praise the

Lord." You'd see the same spirit in the gusto of Brother Jimmy, and the quiet faithfulness of Sister Pete. Faith was demanded by, fostered, and nurtured by our leaders, Deacon and Mother Coleman, who lived it out before us with true grit, and steady determination.

My mother-in-law, Evangelist Stewart, during bootcamp was one of my most ardent supporters, and at the same time one of my greatest challengers. No matter what it was, if she wasn't sure or it wasn't clear, I would have to make it make sense to her. In the early years it was hard, but one day I heard her explaining to my father-in-law and sister-in-law what was going on in church, and the lights came on.

I began to appreciate her insistence that I make plain every step of God's direction for the church under my stewardship. She once told me, if I could not explain it, then it couldn't be from God. That has made so much sense to me, and has clarified my God-given vision to this day.

Through the challenges of their lives and the trials faced by the church, the saints demonstrated that faith was not merely an intellectual exercise. No, it was a deeply personal experiential walk. They taught me that faith is not confined to the walls of the church but that faith informs the life and actions of the believer.

As my church bootcamp years drew to a close, I began to realize the invaluable lessons from these saints concerning living this apostolic walk of faith. It enables us to consistently move forward and take new ground for Christ. This has left an indelible mark on my heart.

The Community of Faith

So, looking back, I can say that the church bootcamp years were some of the best years of my ministry. This experience leads me to highlight the importance of living in a community of faith.

I am profoundly convinced that we are not meant to walk this journey of faith alone. Hebrews 10:25 reminds us to stay connected as a community of believers, "Not forsaking the assembling of ourselves together, as the manner of some is; but exhorting one another: and so much the more, as ye see the day approaching." When we gather together with other believers for corporate worship or simply to fellowship, we have the opportunity to encourage one another, share our struggles, and lift each other up in prayer. In doing so, we strengthen one another and build up the body of Christ.

In the most difficult of times, it has been the relationship with other believers that encouraged me to trust God. Because I was keenly aware that others were looking to me to see how I would handle each crisis, I clung to the Word of God more than at any other time in my life. It was the expectation of my Christian family that challenged me to hold on to my faith. Studies have shown that social support and community can have a positive effect on our mental health and overall well-being. Being part of a vibrant community provides a sense of belonging, is a buffer against isolation and loneliness, and offers a space for growth and learning.

The Early Church Model

The early church as described in Acts 2 provides an excellent example of what fellowship and community can look like in practice. This growing community of new believers devoted themselves to the apostles' teaching, fellowship, the breaking of bread, and prayer. They met together regularly with glad and sincere hearts and their oneness was so strong, many even sold their possessions and gave to those in need. This caring attitude not only built up the community but also attracted new believers so that *"the Lord added to the church daily such as should be saved"* (Acts 2:47). By living as a community and supporting one another, they were able to grow in their faith and share it with others.

In our modern day, in addition to church services, there are many ways to engage in fellowship and community. Joining a small group or bible study, volunteering at a local charity, or participating in the social activities of a faith-based organization are just a few. Through all these seemingly routine activities, never forget that there is a spiritual dynamic at work that I am very conscious of in my role as pastor of a growing congregation. We are all part of the body of Christ, and we each have a unique role to play in building up, supporting, and encouraging one another on our faith journey.

May we all emulate such implicit trust in God, knowing that even in the worst of times, His grace is sufficient, and His love is steadfast!

CHAPTER 3

Overcoming Doubt

> *Ultimately, overcoming doubt requires us to choose faith over fear, and to trust in God's promises even when they may seem unlikely or difficult to believe.*

As humans, we are all prone to doubt and uncertainty. When troubles come, we question our abilities, our decisions, and even our belief system. This doubt can be particularly challenging when it comes to faith.

How can we hold fast to our beliefs when we are confronted by just the opposite reality? After years of serving and increasing my faith, suddenly life happens and causes us to challenge and question everything we were once so certain about.

A Calamity

This is what happened when our worship facility was destroyed by fire. The first reaction to this devastating news was to try and understand how this could happen in the spiritual realm, and what it meant. As the pastor, the first thing I did was to examine myself and then the congregation. Questions began to bombard my mind. Was it I that was not doing something right or was it the congregation? And here's the hard one: "Why God? How could You let this happen?" But the plain truth is we live in a fallen world, and things simply happen.

We are not alone in our searching and questioning. The Bible offers many examples of individuals who struggled with doubt and uncertainty when they could not see the promises of God manifested.

In the Book of Genesis, Abraham and Sarah doubted God's ability to give them a child and took matters into their own hands. So, Abraham had a child through Sarah's handmaid to ensure an offspring. Their doubt and impatience led to untold consequences when that child, Ishmael, grew up in conflict with the real child of promise, Isaac.

The writer of Hebrews stresses how everything we think or do starts with faith: *"And without faith it is impossible to please him, for whoever would draw near to God must believe that he exists and that he rewards those who seek him"* (Hebrews 11:6 ESV). This verse tells us that faith is essential in our relationship with God, and that belief in His existence and goodness is the foundation upon which everything rests.

Overcoming Doubt

So how do we strengthen our faith and overcome doubt? The first thing is through prayer and meditation. Taking the time to pray and meditate on the Word can help us deepen our understanding of the ways of God and our connection with Him.

We have seen earlier how we can also draw from the support of others in our faith community, who can offer perspective and encouragement. When the fire happened, doubt and fear assailed my mind and threatened to overwhelm me. But, once I had spent some time in prayer and meditation with God and received comfort from my congregation, I was strengthened by God's fresh direction. Because of my renewed faith, I was certain that God was ultimately in control of the situation and that, as stated in Romans 8:28, *"all things work together for good to them that love God, to them who are the called according to his purpose."*

Now I don't want you to feel guilty when doubt attacks you because doubts and questions are a natural part of the faith process. As we grow and learn, our beliefs may shift and change, and that is okay. What is most important is that we continue to press into our relationship with God and be totally frank with Him concerning our doubts and waywardness. However, even though it is natural to doubt at first, do not let doubt linger for long. Deal with it quickly because doubt is an enemy of faith and one of the greatest obstacles to a faith-filled life. When we doubt ourselves, others, or our beliefs, it can be difficult to maintain a positive mindset and hold onto our faith when adversity strikes.

Just as we saw how doubt caused individuals like Abraham and Sarah to make serious blunders, the Bible offers other examples of individuals who overcame doubt through their faith. This includes the very same Abraham, who trusted in God's promise of a son and becoming the father to the nations even when that seemed impossible.

We also learn a lesson from Jesus' disciple, Thomas, who wanted tangible proof that Jesus had risen from the dead before he would believe, *"Unless I see in his hands the mark of the nails, and place my finger into the mark of the nails, and place my hand into his side, I will never believe"* (John 20:25 ESV). When Jesus came to them, He instructed Thomas to put his finger in His nail-pierced hands and place his hand on His sword-pierced side. Only when Thomas did so, was he convinced it was Jesus. Then Jesus said to him, *"Have you believed because you have seen me? Blessed are those who have not seen and yet have believed"* (John 20:29). Blessed are we who believe without seeing, for we move by faith and not by sight!

One practical way to overcome doubt is to keep our mind focused on the evidence of God's faithfulness in our lives in our own breakthroughs and the testimonies of others around us. We can also seek out the support and encouragement of others who share our faith, and who can offer us guidance when we struggle with uncertainty. Another important part of my learning and growth was to understand the role of grace in the body of Christ. This expanded my faith from simply cooperating with God to developing greater intimacy with Him. By embracing the role of faith in overcoming doubt, we can cultivate a stronger and more resilient faith, and draw closer to God. Ultimately, overcoming doubt requires us to choose faith over fear, and to trust in God's promises even when they may seem unlikely or difficult to believe.

Above all, since we have a living relationship with Him, we can trust in His goodness, and His promise that He will never leave us nor forsake us. This is how we can cultivate a mindset of joyful expectation that allows us to face life's twists and turns with confidence and hope. It's all about relationships as we shall see in the next chapter.

> *Remember, when you pray, it is you talking to God, and when you read His Word, that is God talking to you.*

Faith is not something that can be attained through sheer willpower or positive thinking; rather, faith is something supernaturally given to us. It is both a gift and a fruit of the Holy Spirit that must be exercised and nurtured over time (See 1 Corinthians 12:9; Galatians 5:22).

One of the most effective ways to strengthen our faith is by spending time with God in earnest prayer and reading God's Word. Remember, when you pray, it is you talking to God, and when you read His Word, that is God talking to you.

It's a running conversation which is the basis of any real relationship. Take note that a real crisis in your life will make this time with God more meaningful and much more impactful.

For me, this time of profound growth in my faith happened when I fell out of the will of God. You heard me right: it was when I fell out of God's will. While I was pastoring, I got into an inappropriate relationship that produced two children while dealing with a marriage on the brink of failure. Yes, you read it right! I have two wonderful children outside my marriage.

Prayer and the Word

As you can imagine, falling out of the will of God was a really difficult time for me. On the one hand, I saw myself as a spiritual "Mike Tyson" who could never be knocked off the religious self-righteous perch I had created for myself. On the other hand, this moral failure made me question my standing with God—even if I was still saved. Remember, the bootcamp had taught me that holiness gave you a right to God's blessings. But this fall had caught me totally off guard, so without holiness where was my standing with God? Fortunately for me, I had nowhere to find help except to come back to God with all my heart.

I spent time in the Word looking at Bible characters I could identify with, including Job, Abraham, and David. I went from praying three times a day to praying all day. I was trying to find myself in God and deal with the pressures of being a man—with all the complications it involved— while at the same time trying to be sure that I was still a man of God. However, it seemed I was losing the battle because I did not understand the message of grace. That message of grace could not come to life until I spent enough time talking to and being talked to by God. But boy when it did come to life, what a great revelation! But it would require all the faith that I could muster to hold on and keep doing the work of God.

There I was with a new understanding that my righteousness was never the catalyst for the move of God in my life. It would always come back to the fact that I had been chosen by an omniscient God who always knew who I was, and that I was never deserving of His blessings. He blessed and kept me simply because I was His child with all my flaws and shortcomings. This became the most impactful time of communicating with God. I developed a relationship that possessed such great understanding about my Father that I could say with the apostle Paul, *"For to me to live is Christ, and to die is gain"* (Philippians 1:21).

Through prayer, we communicate directly with God and seek His guidance and wisdom. We demonstrate our trust and reliance on God, and we open ourselves up to His grace and blessings. It is in this space that we bring up the silent questions and fears that trouble our hearts. In prayer, we give to God our vulnerable selves and those secret truths that we would and could never give to man. In desperate earnest prayer to God, we reveal the cracks in our character, find our true identity in Christ, and pull down the false image we have put out for the world to see. We can simply become that dependent child again that holds who we really are, hidden and never for others to see.

In the Bible, we are encouraged to *"pray without ceasing"* (1 Thessalonians 5:17), and to bring all of our concerns and worries to God. I can tell you that life's biggest challenges and circumstances catapult you into constant prayer. When the complexities of your situation consume your every thought, your every other thought will be towards God. Once you go through such a life-changing event, you make prayer a regular part of your daily life; you create a space for God to work in your life. With that invitation, He is gracious enough to strengthen your faith.

While prayer is you talking to God, reading is God talking to you. Through the pages of scripture, you learn about God's character, His promises, and His plan for your life. Here you can find encouragement and guidance in times of doubt or difficulty, and you can be inspired by the faith of those who have gone before you. Even though Abraham and David themselves made serious mistakes, they were always mindful of their covenant relationship with the Father and found their way back to Him. That greatly encouraged me.

In the book of Romans, we are told that *"faith cometh by hearing; and hearing by the Word of God"* (Romans 10:17). By regularly reading and meditating on the Word, we can increase our understanding of God's will and His ways, and we can be transformed by the renewing of our minds (See Romans 12:2).

Now, spending time with God in prayer and reading His Word is not simply a religious ritual we do out of obligation. On the contrary, it's a powerful way to build and strengthen your faith. By making prayer and Bible reading a regular part of your life, not only can you deepen your relationship with God, but you can also experience the peace, joy, and fulfillment that come from living a life of genuine faith.

In John 1:1-3, we find this amazing statement:

> *In the beginning was the **Word**, and the **Word** was with God, and the **Word was God**. The same was in the beginning with God. All things were made by **him**; and without **him** was not any thing made that was made.*

This passage identifies Jesus as the Word, who was with God from the beginning and who was God Himself. Jesus is again identified as the Word in Hebrews 10:7, *"Then said I, Lo, I come (in the volume of the book it is written of me,) to do thy will, O God."*

Many people have the shallow thinking that the Bible is just a collection of stories and moral lessons. Far from that: it is a living and dynamic encounter with God Himself that has the power to change one's entire life. By seeing the Word as God Himself, as revealed in John 1:1-3, we can approach the Bible with a sense of reverent awe. We can recognize that, through its pages, we have the opportunity to encounter the living God, who created the universe and who desires to be in relationship with us.

In the last pages of the book of Revelation, we are given a glimpse of the future, where God's dwelling place will be among His people:

> *And I heard a great voice out of heaven saying, Behold, the tabernacle of God is with men, and he will dwell with them, and they shall be his people, and God himself shall be with them, and be their God (Revelation 21:3).*

Spending time with God in prayer and reading His Word is surely a rehearsal for the time we will be in His presence forever. When we make time for God in our daily lives, we come face-to-face with Him, and prepare ourselves for the time when we will be with Him forever.

Amazing Grace

Now back to my story. When I found myself unsure of my relationship with God, I became desperate to hold on to Him at all costs. If my world was going to fall apart, I was going to need God especially if I had nothing solid to lean on. During that time, I prayed and read scripture out of personal despair. I began to discover that His grace was there both in times when we were close and when I had fallen out of His will. You see, He had already made provision for me to come back. He died for all my sins past, present, and future. Because of such great mercy extended to me, I could no longer run away and hide. I was drawn to Psalm 51, where David repented of his adultery with Bathsheba, and that became my prayer of repentance too. That gave me the courage to accept responsibility for what I had done, and the resolve to be the best man of God that I could be.

Because I have wonderful children that I love, I am assured that God was not shocked by my indiscretion, but my children are precious to Him. As with one of my children named Jeremiah, before God formed him and each of my children in their mother's womb, He knew and ordained them for their purpose (Jeremiah 1:5). I will forever remind them that they are fearfully and wonderfully made (See Psalm 139:14). As I prayed for them and watched them develop into adults, my faith in God's control over all things has only been reinforced. There was no way I could write a book about my faith and not include one of the most powerful influencers of my faith, my wonderful children—all five of them!

CHAPTER 5

Faith in Action

FAITH THAT CAN MOVE MOUNTAINS

> *Actively living out our faith and putting it into action means serving others, sharing the gospel, and living a life that honors God.*

We've said that faith is not just a belief system; it's a way of life. As James 2:17 (NIV) says, *"Faith by itself, if it is not accompanied by action, is dead."* In other words, faith without the accompanying works is just talk.

Faith requires action. It demands that we live out our beliefs in tangible ways. We cannot simply talk about our faith or believe in it passively. We must actively demonstrate it through our actions and choices. In good and bad circumstances, we must be led by faith, by what we believe God is leading us to or through.

Growing up I remember a young woman who got sick and refused medical treatment. She was what we called at the time a "holiness" church member. The community was in an uproar at her decision; some wanted to blame the preacher or her family. Being her neighbor and a little younger than she was, I had no hesitation in asking her why she did not just seek the doctor's help. I will never forget her answer. She told me that she was saved and that her life was not like anyone else's life. She said she was prepared for whatever God wanted for her life. She believed that God would heal her body, but if He didn't, she would go to heaven, her ultimate goal. I prayed really hard for my friend, Patty. Here was someone who lived out her faith to the fullest with her whole life, and that really impacted my faith.

Jesus emphasized the importance of faith in action when He said, *"Not everyone who says to me, 'Lord, Lord,' will enter the kingdom of heaven, but only the one who does the will of my Father who is in heaven"* (Matthew 7:21 NIV). I heard somewhere that the most important two days in a man's life are when he is born, and when he realizes why. That is indeed a statement of purpose, and true purpose is in doing the will of the Father.

Living out your faith requires you to take risks and step out in obedience to God. It requires you to be bold and courageous in the face of opposition and adversity. It means trusting God even when the path ahead seems uncertain or rough.

Serving and Sharing

One of the best ways to put our faith into action is by serving others. As Jesus said, *"Truly I tell you, whatever you did for one of the least of these brothers and sisters of mine, you did for me"* (Matthew 25:40 NIV). When we serve others, we are demonstrating our love for God and our willingness to show His love to others as He commands.

Another way to live out our faith is by sharing it with others. As followers of Christ, we are called to be ambassadors of His message of love and redemption. We can share our faith with others through living a life that reflects our beliefs.

In his second letter to the Corinthians, Paul writes:

> *You yourselves are our letter, written on our hearts, known and read by everyone. You show that you are a letter from Christ, the result of our ministry, written not with ink but with the Spirit of the living God, not on*

> *tablets of stone but on tablets of human hearts (2 Corinthians 3:2-3 NIV).*

This passage makes the point that our lives testify to others the reality of our faith. We are living epistles, constantly being read by those around us. Our words, actions, and choices all communicate a message about who we are and what we believe.

Additionally, 1 Timothy 4:10 (NIV) states, *"That is why we labor and strive because we have put our hope in the living God, who is the Savior of all people, and especially of those who believe."* We are not only living epistles but also first partakers of the faith that we profess. That is why you will often hear pastors and teachers say they are preaching to themselves.

Living Out Our Profession of Faith

At the beginning of 2023, I introduced a sermon series titled "Living the Good Life" based on Romans 8:28 with no clue that our church would have this catastrophic fire the same month.

The church building was a total write-off with less than adequate insurance coverage. It also had a mortgage to pay, and inflation had skyrocketed. To give you a sense of how high, a dozen eggs hit an all-time high of over $11 dollars in some areas. Our mortgage company wanted us to use their contractors for the building construction, so we needed to raise a quarter of a million dollars just to complete the church restoration. I could not, for the life of me, see any good in a rebuilding project that would put us more in the red.

On top of that, there was Covid. I survived, but my eldest sibling, whom I idolized, did not. I also lost my oldest niece and her mother, my only sister – that was my heart. I lost a dear nephew, who was a pastor I mentored throughout his ministry. I also close my two businesses, catapulting myself into financial strain. I even had to close two of my businesses due to the shutdown. It was a challenging year and a half, to say the least! All these challenges climaxed with the church fire. While I was convinced that I was in the right place doing the right things, these tragedies certainly shook my faith.

The irony was I was writing this book and had launched a new preaching series titled "Life in the All Things" based on a study of Romans 8:28. Here I was preaching and teaching Romans 8:28, *"And we know that all things work together for the good of those who love God, to them that are the called according to His purpose,"* when needless to say, this was not the "all things" that I was expecting from the scriptures.

There I was stuck between the present reality preaching that all things were working together for me to bring about good while at the same time I was covered by catastrophic events. But even in my totally shaken state, I knew that God had to be in charge. I just kept declaring the verse *"all things work together for the good …"* I just kept telling myself that, if I loved God and was called according to His purpose, then anything that was not for *"the good"* was not from God. I just kept looking for the good in everything to find the path of God. And God revealed His will through the lessons: "Use the insurance money to pay off the church, become debt-free, and take all the time needed to rebuild." That was *"the good"* that Romans 8:28 was speaking of.

So, I paid off our church loan at the very time that we needed the money to rebuild. Who does that? Although I was filled with some level of fear and uncertainty, I chose to be bold. What if the members left me or we did not raise enough to rebuild? Well, both of those fears actually materialized; but God is faithful. It was in the uncertainty of my own ability to make things happen that God showed His power to do the miraculous, using only His power to change the hearts of men.

The instances of God coming through are too numerous to mention but one incident stands out. We needed about $7K in plywood, and the chance of raising the additional funds in the time needed was not going to happen because the congregation was stretched and giving sacrificially already. But somehow, I managed to find a huge supply for about half the normal price and I was trying to take advantage of it before it was gone. I did all I could that Friday but to no avail; I just could not raise the sum.

On the following Monday when I went to make the purchase, they told me that I had to wait because the plant manager wanted things moved around the plant. He was so rude and dismissive that, if I didn't need a deal on the plywood, I would have left. Finally, both of us had enough of waiting, and on top of that, his heart was so hardened towards his staff that he ordered them to get the stacks of plywood out of his plant.

In the end, they sold me $7K worth of plywood for less than $300. Yeah, $280, in fact! I was glad I didn't react to the manager's tone of voice.

To make a long story short, we paid off the church and pitched a tent. We renovated the building debt-free and burned the mortgage, while the church continued to keep functioning and growing. Faith moves mountains or mortgages.

The Church as the Solution

So, our faith is not just about what we believe, but also about how we live our lives. When the nation was shutting down during Covid in 2020, I was convinced that we had to live out 2 Chronicles 7:13-14, that is, stand in the gap for our fellowmen:

> *If I shut up heaven that there be no rain, or if I command the locusts to devour the land, or if I send pestilence among my people; If my people, which are called by my name, shall humble themselves, and pray, and seek my face, and turn from their wicked ways; then will I hear from heaven, and will forgive their sin, and will heal their land.*

So, I labeled our church leaders as "essential workers." I opened every day at noon for the sick to come and get prayer. You see, I simply believed that, if there was a pandemic killing people all over the world, then the church had to be the solution.

We could pray as well as minister healing to the sick, leading many to Christ. Again, James 2:14-17 says:

> *What doth it profit, my brethren, though a man say he hath faith, and have not works? can faith save him? If a brother or sister be naked, and destitute of daily food, And one of you say unto them, Depart in peace, be ye warmed and filled; notwithstanding ye give them not those things which are needful to the body; what doth it profit? Even so faith, if it hath not works, is dead, being alone.*

Faith can move mountains or keep you through COVID. Actively living out our faith and putting it into action means serving others, sharing the gospel, and living a life that honors God. Our actions should reflect the love of Christ and point others to Him.

CHAPTER 6

The Science of Faith

FAITH THAT CAN MOVE MOUNTAINS

> *By cultivating a strong sense of faith and purpose, we may be able to improve our overall health and well-being, as well as experience greater peace, joy, and fulfillment in our lives.*

Proverbs 23:7 is such a key scripture, *"For as he thinketh in his heart, so is he."* It emphasizes the power of our thoughts to shape our attitudes, beliefs, and actions, and ultimately to determine the course of our lives. Even the ancient philosopher, Confucius, said, *"The man who says he can, and the man who says he cannot ... are both correct."*

Negative and self-defeatist thoughts can lead to feelings of fear, doubt, and anxiety, while positive life-affirming thoughts build confidence, hope, and resilience. When we place our thoughts under the truth of God's Word, we can experience transformation and renewal that lines up with Romans 12:2: *"And be not conformed to this world: but be ye transformed by the renewing of your mind, that ye may prove what is that good, and acceptable, and perfect, will of God."* By filling our minds with positive and uplifting thoughts from the Word, we can build a mindset of faith, hope, and love. Let us strive to align our thoughts with the truth of Proverbs 23:7, and allow His Word to renew our minds, transform our lives, and shape us into the people He created us to be.

Faith and Health

The connection between faith and the body has been studied extensively over the years, with many researchers exploring how our beliefs affect our physical brains and bodies. Studies have shown that faith can have a powerful impact on both our physiology and psychology, affecting everything from our mood and stress levels to our immune function and longevity.

After my oldest brother had experienced multiple strokes, he came to live with me, where he gave his life to God at the age of sixty-six years old. To God be the glory! With his failing health, he could be heard praying with earnestness and hope. I constantly talked to him to seek God's healing. One day he blew my mind when he admitted he had not yet learned how to use his faith because he did not have enough experience in exercising it. He said he was trying to trust God for "little things" like moving his legs or arms!

One of the most interesting findings is the way in which our beliefs can influence our brains. For instance, studies have shown that prayer and meditation can lead to changes in the brain's structure and chemistry, including increased activity in areas associated with empathy, compassion, and emotional regulation.[1] Additionally, belief has been shown to affect our body's stress response. Studies have also found that people with strong faith or a sense of purpose tend to experience lower levels of stress; hence they have lower levels of inflammation and cortisol, a stress hormone that can have negative effects on the body over time.[2]

One's belief has also been linked to improved health outcomes. Studies have found that people who have a strong faith or sense of purpose tend to have better physical and mental health, as well as greater resilience during times of adversity. The science of faith suggests that belief can have a profound impact on our bodies and minds. By cultivating a strong sense of faith and purpose, we may be able to improve our overall health and well-being, as well as experience greater peace, joy, and fulfillment in our lives.

Navigating a spiritual crisis can be a challenging and even painful experience. However, by seeking support, engaging in spiritual practices, and remaining open to growth and transformation, we can overcome these challenges and emerge with a stronger, more resilient faith.

Turning around Difficult Situations

Romans 8:28 can be difficult to understand, especially when we are going through tough times. However, it is important to remember that this verse does not mean that everything that happens to us will be good or that God causes all of our hardships. Rather, it means that God always turns even the most difficult situations for our ultimate good.

One way to understand Romans 8:28 is to consider the larger context of the passage. In the preceding verses, Paul writes about the struggles and suffering that we may face as followers of Christ. He acknowledges that these trials can be painful and difficult, but he also notes that they are temporary and that they pale in comparison to the glory that is to come.

In light of this, we can understand that even our most challenging experiences can be used by God to shape and refine us. This will make us more like Christ and prepare us for the ultimate goal of our salvation—a new man in Christ. In other words, God can take the broken pieces of our lives and reassemble them to create something more beautiful and meaningful than the original.

It is therefore important to note that Romans 8:28 is not a guarantee that everything will work out exactly as we hope, or in the time we expect. Rather, it is a statement of faith and trust in God's ultimate sovereignty and goodness. When we love God and seek to live according to His purpose, we can trust that even in the midst of hardship and uncertainty, God is working all things together for our good.

CHAPTER 7

Enduring Faith

FAITH THAT CAN MOVE MOUNTAINS

> *So, as we face challenges, we have a choice to make: either allow our circumstances to shake our faith or shape our faith.*

The story of Job is the quintessential testament to the power of faith in the face of catastrophe. Job was a righteous man who faced unimaginable suffering when he lost everything he had, including his wealth, his children, his dignity, and his health. Despite his intense trials, Job did not give up on his faith. He continued to trust in God's faithfulness, even when he did not understand why he was going through so much pain.

Job's story teaches us that perseverance is key to overcoming obstacles. In the midst of his suffering Job said, *"Though he slay me, yet will I trust in him"* (Job 13:15). Such a resolute stance of trust and faith in God helped Job to endure his trials and emerge with his faith strengthened.

We too can take inspiration from Job's example and remember to hold on to our faith when facing obstacles in our own lives.

Limiting God

While many often praise Job for his steadfast faith amid so much suffering, there is an aspect of his story that is often overlooked. You see, satan challenged God, claiming that Job would curse God if his possessions and health were taken away. Some may assume that Job did indeed curse God when he lamented the day he was born and questioned God's justice. Even his wife told him to curse God and die! But Job's words, though full of despair, did not cross that line.

Yet, it is crucial to note that God did rebuke Job for indeed speaking without knowledge or understanding. In response to Job's questioning, God pointed out the vastness of His creation including the intricate nature of His creatures, and asked where Job was when all this was formed.

When confronted with the vastness and sheer magnificence of all this, Job was speechless. All he could say was, *"Behold, I am vile; What shall I answer You? I lay my hand over my mouth"* (Job 40:4 NKJV).

Ultimately, Job repented for having such a limiting view of God, and humbly submitted to God's sovereignty. Then, as God commanded, when he forgave and interceded for his judgmental friends, his fortunes were restored twice as much.

The Value of Perseverance

The apostle James tells us to welcome our trials because their fruit is patience:

> *My brethren, count it all joy when you fall into various trials, knowing that the testing of your faith produces patience. But let patience have its perfect work, that you may be perfect and complete, lacking nothing (James 1:2-4 NKJV).*

Now patience or perseverance is one of the nine fruit of the Holy Spirit. According to the Amplified version, patience is not just the ability to wait, but the manner in which we wait:

> *But the fruit of the Spirit [the result of His presence within us] is love [unselfish concern for others], joy, [inner] peace, patience [not the ability to wait, but how we act while waiting], kindness, goodness,*

faithfulness, gentleness, self-control (Galatians 5:22-23 AMP).

Why is it so important to possess patience or perseverance? In God's eyes, it's the quality that builds character, and character in turn builds hope. This is confirmed in Romans 5:3-4, *"And not only so, but we glory in tribulations also: knowing that tribulation worketh patience; and patience, experience; and experience, hope."*

When we face our trials and tribulations with resilience, it helps us to mature and look with renewed hope towards the future. So, as we face challenges, we have a choice to make: either allow our circumstances to shake our faith or shape our faith.

We can choose to hold fast to what we believe and trust God for what He promises. When we choose to endure and hold fast to our faith, even in the midst of trials and difficulties, we are strengthened and encouraged to continue on the journey of faith.

Each round of faith that we endure can therefore serve as a building block, strengthening our foundation and giving us greater confidence in

God's faithfulness. As we look back on past challenges that we have faced, we can see how our faith has grown and matured, and we are encouraged to continue on the journey of faith.

Ultimately, enduring faith is not just about our own personal growth and development, but also about being a witness to others. As we walk through trials with faith and trust in God, we become a testimony to the power and goodness of God and a source of encouragement to those around us.

So let us hold fast to our faith, persevere through the challenges and difficulties, and trust in the goodness and faithfulness of our God.

CHAPTER 8

Living a Life of Faith

> *As we spend time in prayer and meditate on God's Word, we begin to recognize His voice and discern His will for our lives more clearly.*

Faith is not just a belief system that is confined to religious activities, but it is a way of life that affects every aspect of our existence. This chapter discusses the importance of faith in our daily lives and how it can bring about positive changes.

Helps Us Overcome Fear and Anxiety

In times of uncertainty and distress, faith can be a source of comfort and strength. When we trust in a higher power, our Almighty God, we can find the courage to face our fears and anxieties.

The Bible tells us in 2 Timothy 1:7, *"For God hath not given us the spirit of fear, but of power, and of love, and of a sound mind."* Faith in such promises as this can help us to overcome our fears and face challenges with confidence.

Gives Us a Sense of Purpose

One way that faith helps us overcome obstacles is by giving us a sense of purpose and meaning. When we have faith in something, we know that there is a deeper purpose beyond the challenges we face and that there is a greater plan at work. Believing that we are part of a bigger plan can inspire us to live our lives with greater intentionality and direction.

As Proverbs 16:3 says, *"Commit thy works unto the Lord, and thy thoughts shall be established."* When we purpose to align our actions with our faith, we can find meaning and purpose in our daily lives.

Promotes Compassion and Empathy

Faith can also encourage us to show compassion and empathy towards others. When we believe in a God who loves us unconditionally, it can inspire us to extend that same love and kindness to others.

1 John 4:7 tells us, *"Beloved, let us love one another: for love is of God; and every one that loveth is born of God, and knoweth God."* Faith can help us to see the image of God in others and to treat them with kindness and respect.

Promotes Positive Relationships

When we share a common belief system, it can provide a sense of community and belonging. Hebrews 10:25 encourages us to gather together as a community of believers to support one another, *"Not forsaking the assembling of ourselves together, as the manner of some is; but exhorting one another: and so much the more, as ye see the day approaching."* Attending church services and gatherings can provide opportunities to connect with others who share our faith and values.

Helps Us to Develop Our Relationship with God

As we continue to exercise faith in our daily lives, we not only grow in our ability to trust and rely on God, but we also deepen our relationship with Him. When we trust God to guide and provide for us, we demonstrate our belief in His love, wisdom, and power. Furthermore, as we witness His faithfulness in action, our faith is strengthened and our connection with Him grows stronger. Through faith, we also come to know God better. The more we seek Him and trust Him, the more we understand His character and the way He works.

As we spend time in prayer and meditate on God's Word, we begin to recognize His voice and discern His will for our lives more clearly. And as we follow His leading and obey His commands, we experience the joy and fulfillment that come from living in harmony with His purposes. In short, faith is not just a means of receiving blessings and overcoming challenges, but a vital component of our relationship with God. As we learn to trust Him more fully, we open ourselves up to the transformative power of His grace and the deepening of our spiritual walk with Him.

Provides Hope for the Future

Finally, when we believe in a God who is in control, it can give us confidence that there is a purpose and plan for our lives. Jeremiah 29:11 says, *"For I know the thoughts that I think toward you, saith the Lord, thoughts of peace, and not of evil, to give you an expected end."* Faith can help us to look to the future with hope and optimism, even in the face of adversity. In conclusion, faith is an essential component of our daily lives that can provide comfort, purpose, and hope. By incorporating our faith into our daily routine and interactions with others, we can experience the many benefits that come with a life of faith.

CHAPTER 9

Possessing High Impact Faith

FAITH THAT CAN MOVE MOUNTAINS

> *High impact faith changes the way we live and view God's activities in the world. It allows us to show others, God, in a tangible way and in real time.*

In this chapter, we will explore the concept of possessing high impact faith and the power of speaking into existence the things that are not as though they were, as inspired by Scripture.

In Romans 4:17 God tells Abraham, *"As it is written, I have made thee a father of many nations, before him whom he believed, even God, who quickeneth the dead, and calleth those things which be not as though they were."* This verse highlights our incredible ability to call into existence with faith things that have not yet been seen or experienced.

The next time you fly on a commercial flight, think how ridiculous Abbas ibn Firnas, the true father of aviation, sounded when he announced he was going to jump off the side of a mountain to fly like a bird. And he did. Everybody knows that the Wright brothers invented the first aircraft, but this ingenious ninth-century engineer is regarded as the first human to fly with the help of a pair of wings made of silk, wood, and real feathers. That's how the concept of aviation began.

Years ago, I was approached about helping a gentleman create a way to sell vehicles totally online. I started to explore the idea but swiftly considered the concept ridiculous. I missed it. Now you can buy your dream car on Carvana and have it delivered within the week.

High impact faith changes the way we live and view God's activities in the world. It allows us to show others, God, in a tangible way and in real time. It's like starting a ministry within a drug-infested community or opening a food pantry with no state or corporate support—just a need. High impact faith also calls us to do extraordinary things to affect the kingdom, not using traditional means, but leaning totally on God to make the provision.

The Basis of Calling Forth Things into Existence

High impact faith is marked by a single-minded belief in God's promises and a boldness to declare and affirm those promises even when circumstances suggest the exact opposite. It is about embracing the truth that our words have creative power, and that, as believers, we can declare into the atmosphere God's truth and His plans for our lives.

So, when we possess high impact faith, we speak with conviction and authority, calling forth the fulfillment of God's promises in our lives. We do not allow fear, doubt, or negativity to dictate our confession. Instead, we choose to declare what God has spoken over us, even if it seems contrary to our present reality.

This type of faith is exemplified in the story of Abraham. Despite his old age and the barrenness of his wife, Sarah, Abraham held on to the promise of God that he would become a father of many nations. The very change of his name from "Abram" ("Exalted Father") to "Abraham" ("Father of the Nations") reflected the power of words. In fact, every time Sarah called him, or people addressed him by the new name, they were unconsciously calling forth the fulfillment of this promise, impossible as it seemed.

Eventually, his faith was rewarded when he became the father of Isaac, and the beginning of a great lineage that can be traced down to Jesus Christ.

Therefore, possessing high impact faith requires us to constantly align our thoughts, words, and actions with God's truth and His promises. It means speaking words of life, victory, and abundance, even when the circumstances dictate otherwise. We refuse to be swayed by the negative reports or limitations of doctors, financial experts, or scholars. Instead, we focus on the limitless power of God to bring about transformation, breakthroughs, and miracles.

All Consuming Faith

However, it is important to note that high impact faith is not merely about making positive affirmations or manipulating circumstances to suit our desires. Instead, it's about making our confession and directing our work to conform to God's will and purposes. It means surrendering to His plan, trusting in His timing, and then, becoming consumed with our part in fulfilling the vision given by our Creator.

In conclusion, possessing high impact faith means believing in God's promises and calling into existence the things that are not as though they were. It is being unwavering in our pursuit of the tangibles in spite of the odds or the opposition spoken against our vision by naysayers.

It is about confidently declaring God's promises over our lives and being relentless in our pursuit of His will in the face of monumental challenges. As we exercise this faith, we position ourselves to witness the supernatural manifestation of God's power and provision in our lives and ministries.

CHAPTER 10

Faith That Demands Opposition

> *Just as resistance exercise strengthens our physical muscles, facing opposition, head on, strengthens our faith muscle. It tests our resolve, refines our character, and deepens our trust in God.*

One Sunday morning while on my way to worship, I was filled by an overwhelming heaviness brought on by thinking about all the setbacks in my life. However, little did I know that these setbacks were merely illusions, disguising themselves as obstacles and seeking to detour my journey. At the heaviest moment, while searching for reason and release, I began to ponder on the awesomeness of what I was believing God for. And then I heard it! First, it was a still small voice, but it began to get louder until it screamed in my spirit, "This kind of faith demands to be challenged!"

In this chapter, we will delve into the concept of possessing a faith so strong that it "demands opposition." It's so strong that it jumps around with as much energy as a child in a classroom trying to get the teacher's attention; so strong that it screams so loud that no one else can hear anything but it. It's a faith that stands out so strong that even Jesus would have to acknowledge that no greater faith is in the land, and that satan can't help but challenge it.

Faith Colliding with Opposition

The story of Jesus' temptations, as recounted in Matthew 4:1-11, demonstrates the clash between faith and opposition. The ultimate adversary, satan, sought to test and undermine Jesus' faith by tempting Him mainly by questioning His identity—"If You are the Son of God …" However, Jesus stood firm, not caving in to his taunts, and exhibiting a faith that demanded opposition.

This account teaches us valuable lessons about the nature of faith and the temptations we face on our own spiritual journey. The account reveals that faith, when genuinely embraced, is bound to encounter opposition because it threatens to bring miracles, signs, and wonders out in the open for all to see. That result would not only bless us but glorify God in the process. Now satan can't have any of that, can he?

My point is the presence of opposition does not indicate a lack of faith, but rather its very existence tells the believer that he is on the right track. When we consider the temptations of Christ, one significant aspect of Jesus' responses was His unyielding commitment to God's Word. Each time satan launched an attack, Jesus countered with "It is written ..." This exemplifies the importance of securing our faith in the truth of God's Word and using it as the fuel to counterattack. This is also our ultimate weapon against satan's missiles.

Jesus' response also demonstrates the necessity of relying on the power of the Holy Spirit during any encounter with the devil and his human agents. It was the Holy Spirit that led Him into the wilderness in the first place to be tested, and it was through the Spirit's guidance and strength that He withstood the temptations. This was a necessary part of His learning experience and maturity.

Likewise, we must lean on the Holy Spirit in our own battles, and hold up our shield of faith, so that we are filled with His wisdom, guidance, and empowerment. It is pointless getting embroiled in an argument with the opposition, for you will most certainly be snared. Let the Holy Spirit be your guide.

Outcomes of a Faith that Demands Opposition

The story of Jesus' temptation exemplifies the outcomes when faith demands opposition. First, it builds and strengthens our faith. Just as resistance exercise strengthens our physical muscles, facing opposition, head on, strengthens our faith muscle. It tests our resolve, refines our character, and deepens our trust in God.

Second, opposition allows us to manifest God's glory. When we stand firm in our faith despite the opposition, we become living testimonies of God's power and faithfulness. Our unswerving trust in Him in the face of an attack becomes a powerful witness to the world, drawing others closer to Him.

Lastly, opposition provides the fuel for spiritual growth and maturity. As we navigate the obstacles, our faith expands and helps us develop a greater capacity to trust God in all circumstances. We begin to live in the "all things" of Romans 8:28, *"And we know that all things work together for good to them that love God, to them who are the called according to his purpose."*

When our faith is challenged, we learn valuable lessons about God's faithfulness, provision, and sovereignty.

Testings Are to Be Expected

The Bible tells us not to be caught off-guard when such things come because they are a necessary part of the testing we must all go through, *"Beloved think it not strange concerning the fiery trial which is to try you, as though some strange thing happened unto you"* (I Peter 4:12). Just as gold is tested by fire, so is our testing necessary to prove the kind of faith we have:

> *Such trials show the proven character of your faith, which is much more valuable than gold—gold that is tested by fire, even though it is passing away—and will bring praise and glory and honor when Jesus Christ is revealed (1 Peter 1:7 NET).*

Of course, while opposition can be intimidating and disconcerting, we must remember that we do not face it alone. God is on our side as Romans 8:31 assures us, *"What shall we then say to these things? if God be for us, Who can be against us?"* He is with us every step of the way, and He equips us with His Word to resist and overcome just as Christ overcame.

FAITH THAT DEMANDS OPPOSITION

Any time you can release an appropriate word against the accuser, you crush his opposition. Therefore, through the power of the Holy Ghost, prayer, and reliance on God's Word, we can maneuver our way through the sea of opposition, emerge with a victorious faith, and raise up a standard against the opposer.

What kind of faith do you want to possess: a faith that can move mountains, produce signs and wonders, and raise the dead or one that is more talk than action? The faith that moves mountains produces the intangibles and demands serious opposition. This level of faith stands strong in the face of challenges and temptations and emerges victorious because it will accept no other possible outcome. Just as Jesus overcame satan's temptations through the power of God's Word and the guidance of the Holy Spirit, we too can cultivate a faith that triumphs over opposition.

Let us embrace these lessons from Jesus' temptations, and develop a faith that is unshakeable, unwavering, and victorious no matter what opposition the enemy brings against us.

CHAPTER 11

Wondrous Faith

FAITH THAT CAN MOVE MOUNTAINS

> *Obedience is an essential component of a faith that works, as it positions us for God's miraculous intervention when all-natural means have been exhausted.*

In this chapter, we will explore the story of the floating ax head from the life of the prophet Elisha, and the episode of Peter walking on water. From here we can extract valuable insights into a faith that truly works, as taught in the Old and New Testaments.

Divine Intervention

The account of the floating ax head in 2 Kings 6:1-7 demonstrates the supernatural intervention of God when genuine faith is exercised. We see how the junior prophets in Elisha's school of the prophets sought the master's help when, by accident, the ax head broke off and fell into the water. Through faith, the seemingly impossible occurred—the iron ax head floated to the surface by means of a stick. This story emphasizes the significance of acknowledging our limitations, seeking divine assistance, and embracing the realm of possibilities that exceed human understanding and expectation. Another remarkable example of faith in action is found in Matthew 14:22-33, where Peter walks on water. When Peter saw Jesus walking on the water, he expressed his desire to join the Master. Jesus invited Peter to come and, as Peter stepped out of the boat, his faith allowed him to walk on water. However, when he shifted his focus from Jesus to the storm engulfing him, he began to sink. In this story, we learn the importance of keeping our eyes fixed on Jesus and maintaining resolute faith, even when the waters of life are turbulent. There will always be opposition to your objective. But when your objective is to glorify God by operating in the realm of the impossible and holding on to your alignment with God's will, you will fix your eyes on God and not look to the right or left.

Suspending Unbelief and Stepping Out

Both stories bring out the significance of obedience to God's specific instructions and demand the suspension of all human reason. The young trainee prophet obeyed Elisha's directive to throw a stick into the water, just as Peter obeyed Jesus' invitation to come to Him. Obedience is an essential component of a faith that works, as it positions us for God's miraculous intervention when all-natural means have been exhausted.

In addition, these narratives reveal that faith often requires stepping out of our comfort zones to achieve the miraculous. The prophet Elisha had to let go of the possibility of ridicule by throwing in the stick and believing in the supernatural power of God to make the ax head defy the laws of water and steel and begin to float. Peter had to leave the safety of the boat and trust that Jesus would enable him to walk on water with the only frame of reference being Jesus walking before his very eyes. A faith that works necessitates stepping beyond what seems reasonable and venturing into the realm of the unknown through trusting God.

The stories of the floating ax head and Peter walking on water also teach us that, for the believing child of God, setbacks and challenges do not have the final say. Just as the ax head sank but was raised to the surface, and Peter sank but was rescued by Jesus, our faith has the power to overcome failure and bring about wondrous victory. It reminds us that in our moments of doubt or fear, Jesus is always there to extend His hand and lift us up—remember, Jesus promised never to leave nor forsake us (See Hebrews 13:5). So when opposition comes—and it will—simply turn your attention back to God, and never consider the opposition at all.

ENDNOTES

1. Retrieved from https://primexaos.com

2. Retrieved from https://ncbi.nlm.nih.gov

ABOUT THE AUTHOR

Dr. James T. Jackson Sr. has been married to his childhood sweetheart, Lady Jackson, for thirty-nine years. They have five wonderful children and nine grandchildren.

Dr. Jackson started his ministry at the age of seventeen as an associate minister at the Greater Shiloh Baptist Church, Danville, IL under the leadership of his beloved pastor, the Late Rev. H.L. Reed. Shortly afterward, he received his first call to the Pastorate at the First Church of Christ, Fostoria, OH, where he grew up as a child. He later became the Pastor of the William Street Church of God, Danville IL, where he served for three years before founding the New Jerusalem Church of Jesus Christ, which he pastored for over twenty-one years. Dr. Jackson has planted seven church ministries and has multiple spiritual sons pastoring churches throughout the country and within Power of Faith Assemblies Worldwide Inc., where he currently serves as presiding prelate.

Dr. Jackson has a degree in Christian Education from Aenon Bible College in Indianapolis, IN, and a Bachelor of Science in Business Management from Shorter University in Rome, GA. In addition, Dr.

Jackson possesses a Master of Practical Theology from Ohio Christian University and a Th.D. in Practical Theology from the American Bible University.

In the midst of a successful business career as an automobile dealer and a licensed financial advisor, Dr. Jackson also dedicated his life to pursuing excellence in ministry with a focus on kingdom-building as a lifestyle.

To contact Bishop Dr. Jackson regarding speaking engagements, please use the information below.

Dr. James T. Jackson
eldjak50@gmail.com
https://www.pffwci.org
404-993-4352

www.ingramcontent.com/pod-product-compliance
Lightning Source LLC
Chambersburg PA
CBHW050322010526
44119CB00003B/70